PACO'S ATLAS AND OTHER POEMS

John Thieme

SETU PUBLICATIONS
Pittsburgh, PA (USA)

Paco's Atlas and Other Poems

By

John Thieme

Setu Publications
* Pittsburgh, PA (USA) *

We would be pleased to receive email correspondence regarding this publication or related topics at setuedit@gmail.com.

ISBN-13 (paperback): 978-1-947403-00-0

Cover Design by Aparajita Sharma

Printed and bound in the United States of America.

Distributed to the book trade worldwide by Setu Publications, Pittsburgh (USA)

Setu Literary Publications, Pittsburgh, USA

Paco's Atlas and Other Poems

By

John Thieme

Acknowledgements

I thank the editors and publishers of the following print and online publications, where poems included in this collection first appeared:

Asia Literary Review

A Warm Mind-Shake: Scritti in onore di Paolo Bertinetti, ed. Carmen Concilio

Coldnoon: Travel Poetics

Muse India

New Academia

Quickfictions

SARE (*Southeast Asian Review of English*)

Setu

Tuck Magazine

Contents

Foreword

Many years ago, as a very young man, I attended one of the most famous cultural events of the so-called "Swinging Sixties", the International Poetry Incarnation, held in London's Royal Albert Hall in 1965. The event is remembered as the night when Allen Ginsberg and the Beat Poets came to town and at short notice the Hall was filled with an audience of 7,000 people. This legendary evening featured performances by seventeen poets who, in varying degrees, embodied the spirit of Sixties counter culture. Ginsberg was indisputably the star.

On the way into the Hall, I saw him giving out flowers, while his acolytes, who included a bevy of women clad in white gossamer, danced attendance, dutifully fanning the master. It seemed the performance had begun before the poetry. Inside, much of the audience, which unbeknown to me is said to have included Indira Gandhi, appeared to be immersed in the mood of hedonism, participants as much as onlookers. In retrospect, I realize that I was a spectator, an amused bystander. Amid all the posturing, one moment left an indelible impression on my mind. It was not Ginsberg intoning two of his longer poems, not Lawrence Ferlinghetti reading "Underwear", not the German poet Ernst Jandl introducing the audience to sound poetry, and not Adrian Mitchell declaiming "To Whom It May Concern" ("Tell Me Lies About Vietnam"). What I remember most vividly is the moment when earnest Harry Fainlight tried to explain what one of his poems was about. He was attacked by members of the gathered fraternity of poets (tellingly, all seventeen were male!) that surrounded him.

They told him simply to read the poem. As I remember it, Ginsberg chanted the words "Read Poem, Read Poem" again and again, but was this Ginsberg or one of the other poets? In any case, poetry, the implication was, speaks for itself. Poetry needs no introductions, no notes, no glossaries. Fainlight, visibly disturbed, persevered, but on that heady marijuana-fuelled night when the Underground annexed this famed Victorian auditorium, he was out of step with the predominant mood. He was roundly defeated by the avant-garde coalition of voices that was thriving on self-dramatization and easy political rhetoric. To be fair, this was a performance occasion, and Ginsberg and company were altogether more entertaining and, needless to say, some of the poetry was very impressive – "To Whom It May Concern" reads well today – but I was left pondering the heart-on-sleeve political blandishments and wanting to ask whether poetry *should* speak for itself, without commentary.

One knows that many readers are eager to know whether poems come out of personal experiences, that they may appreciate superficially obscure passages being elucidated and that they may like to see the dominant issues in a collection signposted. I find it difficult to respond to these wishes, though I can say that very little in *Paco's Atlas* has come directly out of my own experience, even if everything one writes is in a sense a piece of oneself. The two poems about family members included here may appear to be "personal" and one of them, "Grandmother", is loosely based on my own maternal grandmother's life. In contrast, the other, "Uncle", is pure invention. Is there anything else that comes out of my own lived experience? Not that I am aware of, though "The Settlement" was inspired by a brief visit to an Amerindian mission in Guyana and "Tea-Time" by a drive towards Nuwara Eliya in Sri Lanka. Does anything need elucidation? Not for those who know that Saraswati is the Goddess of libraries as well as wisdom more generally; not for those who recognize that in "From Dylan to Dylan", Bob Dylan is talking to Dylan Thomas, from whom he adopted his name; not for those who realize that Marco in "Couple" is Marco Polo. On balance, neither these glosses nor any others seem to add much. The cadences of the poems themselves are the lifeblood of the verse, not the search for sources and background.

I also find it difficult to identify patterns in my work, though I am aware that I return to situations, sometimes trying to address inequities, hopefully with a more inclusive approach than was on display on that supposedly groundbreaking Albert Hall night. An impetus towards political positioning is usually, not always, left in abeyance, for readers to supply it, if they so choose. In "Chinese Checkers", "Couple" and "Tea-Time", Asian women counter their appropriation by Western intruders, but these are very varied intruders: the tourists of "Tea-Time" are comparative innocents, when compared to Marco Polo, whose fabrications I respond to in "Couple". Several of the poems could be seen to relate to my academic work on postcolonial and environmental issues: the title-poem, "Paco's Atlas", chimes with my comments on alternative cartographies; "Tempests" uses the tradition of *le libertinage* to comment on the disastrous effects of climate change. "Pragmatist" and the mini-epic at the end of the collection, "The Tortoisiad", wrestle with the problem of representing animal experience, without anthropomorphizing it. Elsewhere, the dissemination and reception of art and literature is to the fore, particularly in "A New Woman ", which began life as a quick fiction, and "In the Picture". It would be hard to claim any of the poems as orthodox love poems, but "I Watch Her Write", "Courtly Love" and "Vinegar" gesture towards this genre while one of the collection's numerous elegiac poems, "Afterwards", links lost love and ecological ruin.

Castaways have always fascinated me, initially I think because of Dr Johnson's *Dictionary* definition of a castaway as a person lost or abandoned by Providence; later, I suppose, because of my longstanding interest in the poetry of Derek Walcott. But then I have also been alternately fascinated and appalled by novels such as *Robinson Crusoe*, *Treasure Island* and *Lord of the Flies*. "Ben Gunn", an imagined version of my favourite character in Stevenson's novel was a logical emanation of this interest and, when I started to think about the possibility of Indian castaways, it was natural to imagine a version of the apostle St. Thomas, still wracked with doubts, on the Malabar coast.

There are other poems that work as pairs: "Rumours", inspired by Borges' fictions, and "Saraswati" use libraries as tropes to reflect on the shift away from the culture of the book, but I allow them to have very different outcomes. "Nosferatu" and "Et in Arcadia …" assume different positions on vampires, though both evince a degree of nostalgia for what they might be seen to represent.

The poems travel across cultures and attempt something similar on a formal level by moving between varied modes of verse, some regular, some irregular. For me, the neatness of the regular is a way of arbitrarily imposing a version of order; the disjunctions of the irregular a means of conceding that the quest for completion will surely fail. "Another Night" concludes with the archetypal storyteller, Scheherazade, finding a perfect moment, when "the urgency of narrative / drifts into an aimless present". It's a moment I identify with, because it leaves the process of writing ongoing and I find it hard to finalize poems and let them escape to be published, in case I may be able to improve them later. That said, the poems included here have, of course, all found a finished form….

Do I have a favourite among these poems? Yes, it's "The Slaughter", in which two versions of history are juxtaposed in an attempt to unsettle the assertion that "History is written by the victors". In the poem's response to this aphorism, History is a hegemonic discourse controlled by the written word: History is written, but not necessarily by the victors. Oral accounts may convey more truth, but they are usually occluded by the scribal. Inevitably the poems here assume a written form, but in "The Slaughter", "Grandmother" and sections of other poems such as "Couple", I try to counter this by privileging imagined oral voices.

What I've written here may suggest that I have veered towards the Harry Fainlight side of the argument that emerged at the International Poetry Incarnation, but I'm not sure that I want to take that position. Ultimately what I've written here represents little more than a belated attempt to rationalize what I was doing when I wrote the poems and I think I would prefer simply to say, "Read Poem". Most of the pieces were born out of an attempt to dream a particular situation into existence, but such attempts frustrate completion, not just for the reason mentioned above, but also because readers will inevitably be the ultimate arbiters of meaning. Without readers, writing is inert and lifeless. So, I hope that those of you who are about to embark on this short volume will dream with me. Some of the poems ("Another Night", "Pragmatist", "Saraswati") make dreaming explicit, but dreams that endeavour to usher in new modes of perception litter the pages of the whole collection. Amid the dreamt elegies for past times and lost loves ("Nosferatu", "Uncle", "Afterwards") and the longing to remain in a suspended present dreamtime, there is a focus on future possibility and poetry's force as a medium for dreaming alternative ways of thinking into being.

John Thieme
June 2018

Preface

A folio of maps in verse, *Paco's Atlas* shape-shifts and spills over the borders and frames of atlases geographical, ethnographical, anatomical and zoological. It is filled with the wonder, the horror and the irony of maps: surreal dissections, absurd projections, encyclopaedic compressions, the circular logic of treasure-island shorelines that trap Ben Gunn like vampire bats under the sign of Nosferatu. If Mercator's frontispiece Atlas, as Bruno Latour reminds us, transformed the image of the Greek Titan supporting the world on his shoulders into a scientist who held it in his hand, the mapmaker of *Paco's Atlas* places it in the mind of one of his creations, Paco, and through this curious child re-explorer of flattened, yet layered fictions of the world, in that of the reader who can re-imagine John Thieme's *Paco's Atlas* as his or her own. Here, it is the mapped who tell their stories: self-conscious of their roles of "bit-players in an oft-repeated scene" like the tea-pickers in "Tea-Time", they "mark territory" out of Descartes' cogito like the dog in "Pragmatist" and re-imagine, like Paco, many a "book's topography" by correcting its typographical "mistakes". In these retellings, they have the mapmakers inhabit their own cartographic tales as characters and wonder, as in "Settlement", if they are "just another tribe of voyeurs, / intruding on the knowledge of this place" or seek, as in "In-Action", for the "camouflage of home".

Paco's Atlas may also be read as a creative companion or travel guide to John Thieme's work on postcolonial and global literatures – an extensive contribution to the field in both its significance and range. For me, his poetry collection is not only marked by the same passion for revisionist cartographies, but reads also at once, as sophisticated and effortless as his criticism, intellectually rewarding, yet seductive like Scheherazade's tales.

Vassilena Parashkevova

University of Surrey, UK

Paco's Atlas

There are many stories in the flattened maps of Paco's Atlas:
tales of altitudes, temperatures and empires.
Paco loves the undulating greens of the book's topography,
the scorching reds of its tropic heat and the glacial blues of its arctic
cold,
but he detests those pages that speak of wars and politics.
Paco is terrorized by bold primary colours that assert possession,
and maps that hide human histories of love and loss and lassitude.

Paco wakes in the night, screaming at Mercator's madness
and the visions of Heaven and Hell in medieval *mappae mundi*.
He seeks solace in Ptolemy, and ibn-Hawqal's map of earth,
with Mecca at the centre and the south on top.
Paco is reassured to see spaces populated with humour
and to know that west and north are neither here nor there,
but anywhere one cares to put them.
Paco laughs himself to sleep.

Paco wakes in the morning, tetchy and tense again.
He deserts his Atlas to go in search of the ultimate projection,
a map of earth that is neither round nor flat,
but, scratched on stone, spreads lazy rumours of watercourses,
unseen mountain passes and cryptic routes across the sea.
Paco kicks up pebbles, but does not discover *the* stone he seeks.
He finds a boulder that shows the faded outline of a warrior's spear,
thrusting itself into the body of an enemy,
or is this just a farmer threshing corn?

Defeated in his quest, Paco goes home to his Atlas,
turning its pages with the fervour of a man condemned to hang at dusk.
He shreds every section that supports the claims of other explorers.
He annihilates stories of navigation, settlement and greed,
until the Atlas is slimmed down to four blank endpapers.
On the temporary reprieve of this *tabula rasa*,
Paco begins to draw his own cloth of the world,
with Maseratis, toothpicks, Buddhas and eggs in the cartouche.
Paco reinvents Sumatra and Mauritius in the shape of dogs;
Chile becomes plump and purple, with an Atlantic coast
and smiling arms that stretch towards the Bight of Benin.
Paco's Atlas recreates the earth, and the stories start anew.

Rumours
(for Jorge Luis Borges)

Word had had it that there were no books
left in the library of Babel,
but two years back, a green trainee was sent
to find a rumoured yellow relic
of the galaxy of Gutenberg.
A battered text of several thousand pages,
this vellum volume was said to hold the key
to the mysteries of unrestricted space.

Supine on a trestle-mounted crib,
the aged librarian lies lonely in his cell,
the dying nerve centre of a universe of print.
His clouded eyes gaze at newspapered walls,
more interested in the tabloid images pasted there
than reading words of learning, faith or love.

There is no message from the young trainee;
only moths and mice make any sound.
It may be that the acolyte has died of boredom
in the archive's far-flung empty corridors
and the labyrinthine shelves of vacant space.

Beyond the walls of Babel lie the shrinking wetlands,
where, rumour has it, migrant herons
seek water once a decade, not yearly as before,
but this can't be confirmed as fact or fiction:
it's generations since the last apostate
escaped into the realms of feral space,
and sent ten words to those enclosed within.

The librarian's fading mind and senses ramble.
He doubts if there's a world outside his cell.
But now his phone rings and he slowly draws it earwards.
There is a voice, but deafness mutes the call,
a rumour from a ghost, explaining all.

The Slaughter

I: Text

They say that history is written by the victors,
but deep in Amazonis, there lived a tribe
who won every battle, yet never learned to write.

They exterminated their neighbours,
apart from a sole survivor, who escaped to Bahia,
and wrote his epic, *O abate*.
It is our only record of these events,
a saga of his people's countless victories,
written in blood red on rolled parchment scrolls.

Today his manuscript is curated under glass,
a prize exhibit in a national library.
Copies are read in Taiwan, Tunisia and Trinidad.

Os vencedores have lived to tell no tales.
History is written …

II: Testimonio

"Do you have your notebook – OK your keypad –
ready to record my words?
It happened like this,
exactly as I am going to tell you.
Listen carefully.
Transcribe me accurately.

"There was an ambuscade, they used dirty tricks.
We were surprised from trees and bushes.
They had arrows, blowpipes, cutlasses.
But Macunaima favoured our cause,
knowing us to be pure in heart.
He made rain to swell the rivers,
and wash away their boats.
We regrouped, we fought,
and we won this battle, like all the others.
Just one of their vermin escaped in a canoe.
He disappeared forever.

"Did you get all that down, exactly as I said it?
Tell the world, this is how it happened."

The Settlement
(for Wilson Harris)

Leaving a widening vee in our wake,
we throttle through the overhanging bush.
Our outboard engine takes us on to Santa mission,
a settlement established ... who can say exactly when.
Our pilot is part-Arawak; he knows these waters.
His half-shut eyes and supple wrists
negotiate piranha channels in the creek
that swallows lives impartially.

We live within the narrow sea-walled ribbon,
below the level of the ocean's edge,
where kokered Dutchmen built a wooden town,
improbable as sin, or ice amid this tropic heat.
Yet coming here, we do not see ourselves as tourists.
This, after all, is *our* Interior country,
our birthright, too, a refuge from the coast.
Our mothers, cousins and grandfathers,
sowed crops, cut cane, drank rum and ate brown rice.
But as we inch towards the promised haven,
are we just another tribe of voyeurs,
intruding on the knowledge of this place?

At last we reach the mission's scruffy clearing,
beside the stelling in the shallows of the creek,
dyed coca-cola by the vegetation.
We step ashore, home-seekers in this wishful space.
It seems a timeless moment.
The thatched huts may have been constructed
last year, this week, a century ago.
There are no occupants in sight.
Our pilot says these are retiring people,
furtive watchers, seeing while unseen.
So perhaps it will be better if we leave,
before we break the place's codes of silence.

But now a small boy runs out from a hut,
naked from his waist down to his feet,
and a woman, who must be his mother,

follows, stumbling in her chase.
She gathers him within her arms.
and stares at me in fierce defiance.
I fumble to find words that may engage her.
I ask, "Which saint is Santa named for?"
Her shoulders raised, she shrugs with heedless scorn
and answers in the global language:
"We never did have saints and never would have any.
What use could they be in a place like this?
Our days are numbered, but we shall outlive you
by many, many rainy seasons,
and then perhaps we will be settled here."

I Watch Her Write

Scratched scabs, healed wounds, a stockade built of words.
I watch your hand sliver across the azure paper.
Your college teacher called your writing feline.
Perhaps she's right, but leonine seems closer to the mark.

And when you raise your eyes and smile at me,
I sense bold irony amid the cursive letters
of your Cyrillic wisdom, learnt in country towns.
Ignoring all my well-meant questions,
you keep the secret of your silent pages –
calligraphy that speaks the language of your soul.

I long to share the knowledge of your flowing hand.
I dream of entering your wilderness of words
to imitate the echoes of your arcane scrawl,
until from constant mindless repetitions
I learn to speak a woman's body's peace.

Vinegar

Balsamic, matured across the years,
sweetens the dinner jacket of my mind,
but there are also days when, wrapt in chipshop jeans,
I relish the tartness of the commonplace.

Like vinegar, you redeem
an unthanked meal from oblivion.
You bring me all its changing moods,
decanting your flavours with olive oils,
darkening salads, already green with love.

In the Picture
(for Eunice de Souza)

After Katerijn abandoned cubism,
she briefly flirted with surrealism,
before finding her true home in a Dutch interior.
She wandered through Vermeers and Bruegels,
bypassing earrings, lace and a guitar
and the giddy, restive pleasures of the
never-ending war between Carnival and Lent.
Then settled on a well-upholstered chair
in a quiet and restful corner of a Pieter de Hooch.

She stared at captive maps upon the walls,
the trade routes of the world within this room.
She nursed her child, she stroked her cat.
She opened both the shuttered windows,
her portals to the lands inside the maps.

Passers-by were scuttling through the day-long rain,
disturbing puddles with their truant shoes.
The window-framed canal was clogged with weed.
There must, she knew, be more extended ways of living,
for sailors bringing cinnamon to Flanders
from lands where men gave birth to monsters,
but how could such abstraction compete with her still life?

A New Woman

This is the captive portrait of a lady,
pulled from a novel, where she only lived in words.
This is the way the famous artist saw her visage,
rouged cheeks, brown eyes, a mop of hennaed hair.

Her head is tilting to the left-hand side,
as if she's gently asking, "Am I real?"
Her mouth is puzzled to be here in oil.
Like La Gioconda's smile, her troubled grin
attracts the gaze of all who view her shrine:
"These are the dentals of her teeth", one jokes,
"Those are the lazy labials of her lips,
soft consonants, locked in with love."
Another says with equal certainty
that he can hear the vowels of her voice.
Not to be outdone, a freckled nun exclaims,
"She is the perfect mirror of my soul!
I see myself within her plumbless eyes."
Contagion spreads as others catch her mood.
They, too, now find their likeness in her frame.
Like Botticelli's Venus each one steps ashore,
newborn, completed by the *darshan* of her face.

The painter watches, dispossessed and mute.
When he'd invented her, with russet daubed on grey,
he'd planned she would be his alone.
The book had called her wistful, wan and sickly.
She'd been a skin-deep outline unfulfilled,
a slender spectre seeking flesh and bones.
His brushstrokes had transformed her febrile grace;
his art had given substance to a wraith.
Now every pilgrim claims her as their own.
She'll die, infected by their universal love.

Pragmatist

Lately, in that suspended hour,
before I lose myself in the night,
I dream the world as a dog,
sniffing where others have been,
yesterday, last week, a month ago.

Exploring the stinks of yesteryear,
I check grass, stones and gateposts.
Eliminating the unnecessary,
I pick my way through unrecycled crumbs.
I am no ecologist,
but I clean up as I go.

Scouring cemeteries, I detect bones
beneath the urine on the gravestones.
Scavenging amid these granite tributes,
I, too, mark territory.
Man's best friend, I love women too.
Gazing up with hazel, adoring eyes,
I train humans to feed me.
I am the perfect family member.
I make friends with their friends,
I growl discreetly at their enemies.

I swim easily, amphibiously,
disdainful of landlocked cats.
Back on the riverside, I shake myself dry,
and doze with one eye open, one ear cocked.
I snooze at will, but never catnap.
I look to the stars, but I follow my nose.

Outside my dog dream, I am a confirmed doubter,
but in that suspended hour all uncertainty disappears.
I focus on the smells in hand,
I sniff, therefore I am.

Chinese Checkers

I make steady progress across the board.
"Imperious" is the word you use to describe it,
while mounting a nonchalant defence,
against my hopeful, hopping pegs,
pygmy soldiers in the Shanghai dusk.

In a moment of distraction, as I sip my tea,
broken orange pekoe from Sri Lanka,
I venture to remark that China
has given much to the West, and you reply,
"Oh yes, but taken so much more.
You taught us all your rules of trade,
how to give and take. We gave, you took.
That habit will be hard for us to break.
And this game? Japan gave *us* this German game,
so now we make smart sets to send to you."

While you say this, I strive to cross the board
and steal a victory through a pincer-like advance,
hoping that your mind may be wandering to
your husband who left you a year or two ago,
or your lover, arrested for cheating at checkers
with the sharp-faced Russian ambassador,
whose diplomatic immunity saved their skins.

"Of course," you say, "The West has given too,
but let's not talk about the Opium Wars."
There's little humour in your voice.
"One way of avoiding that past
is to put it in the margins of a longer,
finer history of walls and warriors and woks.
Oh yes, we sent you woks too, didn't we?"

The game looks to be moving towards stalemate,
as you pull backwards from the board,
grating your chair-legs on the tiled floor.
I see a chance to win the day
and swiftly push my pegs towards your space.
You deftly thwart my move, not by ingenious defence,
but by rising to your feet. You whisper softly,
"Our pandas seldom mate in Western zoos."

Couple

Marco's spices seduced many Christian palates in the West,
but tired of telling tales about the Orient
he travelled East again – to Cathay, where he'd found his second home.

His mistress eased herself down on him,
silently demanding *her* pound of flesh.
So he told her tales of an amphibious city by the Adriatic,
its rainbow fish, the hunchback bridges of Dorsoduro,
and the beak-nosed boats of the thousand and two canals
that wind their sinuous courses within its boggy lagoon.

Satisfied at length, she uncoupled herself
from his body and his stories
and crossed the room, to reclaim the clothes
she had strewn on the floor in her haste to meet his skin again.
She turned towards the couch, where Marco dribbled on.

"I am", she said, "a credulous woman,
unlike your knowing countrymen.
So please take these garments to them,
as proof of my nakedness when I am with you;
and let them hear the stories you have told me,
so they can judge both whether you possessed me
and whether, like me, they too may be real.
Let them wear my clothes, Marco, but first let me come again.
Be silent, while I invent you as a figment of my dreams,
and keep your stories for the waterfolk."

Tea-Time

Climbing into the high interior of their fancies,
they spiralled towards Nuwara Eliya,
trusting their driver's knowledge of the bends.
Like the villages, the noonday heat receded.

The road corkscrewed through ever greener slopes,
and then, as if to order, they came upon tea-pickers,
sari-clad women with remembered headscarves,
transferred from kitchened packages at home.

"They pluck the leaves," the driver said, "for *peet-ance*."
He told them how the women came to be there,
Tamil migrants from another time and place.
"They work so hard for very little money."

He stopped the car, without their asking, saying,
"You may please take their photo, if you wish,
but first you ask permission, so it's all OK.
You ask Sonali. Wait, I call her here."

A broken-toothed, rough-cheeked imposing woman
approached the car, with proud unflinching eyes.
They pointed at their camera, gestured towards the pickers,
"We'd like a photo, showing them at work."

A rehearsed script came tripping off her tongue.
"No problem. Just take what you wish.
We like to show you how you get your tea.
First you see us, then visit factory."

She nodded at her leaf-stained, outstretched palm,
then spoke three words towards her watching crew.
Still plucking leaves, they flashed accustomed smiles,
bit-players in an oft-repeated scene.

The camera shutter clicked, she took the note they proffered,
with hands made supple by her daily toil.
"Thank you," she said. "Without you we have nothing.
I pray you'll never choke upon our tea."

She turned away and fumbled for her smartphone.
The driver smiled and tossed the coin
Sonali had just slipped him.
He, too, had played a long-familiar part.

Saraswati

I hide.
Behind the unloved cluttered bookshelves,
camouflaged in a dark salwar kameez,
I elude prying eyes,
until my time can come again.

I hide.
Within the sunless north wing of this library,
sixteen padded desks have sixteen cushioned chairs,
where sixteen well-fed scholar gypsies,
my one-time devotees, their eyes made dim by screens,
rush to fill work stations with their games of war.
It's years since they last turned a page.
Their whispered chatter echoes down the hall.
Its echoes pay lip service to my name.

I hide.
I took a vow of silence many years ago.
I gather wisdom in the twilight gloom.
I pace closed corridors at night.
I travel future centuries in dreams.
Concealed behind the shelves,
my thumb-nailed pages clear a space
for the entry of a dog-eared bookworm,
a reborn relic of the world's myopic past.
He will return to read with me again,
vast alphabets of upright types of love.

In-Action

In action on this unforgiving frontier,
where trampled mud obscures a cause unknown,
we never see the women's covered faces.
we never get to look inside their huts.
At dusk I smell tomorrow's sodden sunrise,
the battle fatigue of a futile dawn.
Perhaps we never should have come here,
but statesmen ratified their votive compacts
and I escaped inaction back at home.

One khaki day descends into another
and all their nameless leaders look the same.
No Trojan horses, Mata Haris, Alexanders,
no ersatz wannabe James Bonds,
just the to and fro of aimless rutted roads,
the crackling phone lines and those unseen women,
who traipse, eyes down, towards polluted wells,
invisible behind their seeing veils.

Perhaps we should have stayed within our borders,
adjusting to the camouflage of home.

Ben Gunn

The sun assaults another mindless morning;
a saurian smile is playing round his lips.
He's counting shadows from the fronds of palms.
His half-clenched teeth have lost the urge to speak,
but now he hears a stern, unsettling echo –
his voice returned? It's barking, hoarse and loud.
"Who's there?" But he already knows and why they've come.

They've built a stockade on the western high ground,
the mound where he once slept, for just two nights.
Drenched on the second, he prefers the seashore,
beneath the sand dunes of this leeward hill.
What kind of crazy people must they be,
to settle there, indifferent to wind and rain?

He knows a clearing in the forest's darkness,
where bones decay, becoming one with earth.
Who knows what riches are interred there?
Who knows what ghosts may yet come back to life?
But now grave-robbers will despoil it,
exhuming plunder, buried with a curse.

There are many forms of hidden treasure
and many ways of turning left or right.
He's trodden every inch of his uncharted kingdom.
His greatest insight is to know for certain,
as sure as day succeeds to humid night,
that if you hug the shoreline of the island,
the wandering circle of its broken strand
will always bring you back where you began.

There was a time he'd longed to leave the island,
return to puddings, cheddar, peas and plums.
He'd liberated messages in bottles.
They'd always sunk. He'd cut his foot on glass.
But now he only craves his self-made nation,
no courts, no churches, nor the wrath of laws,
no form of rank or subjugation.
This is that old world's other Eden.

Who would forsake this desert for their towns?

He hears his mouth begin to speak once more,
in rasping tones that cannot be his own:
"Lie low, make sure they don't observe you.
Unseen, you can't be owned again.
They do not share the wisdom of the island,
the knowledge of its moss-strewn forest paths.
They bring their action to inertia,
these cannibals who plan to raid the tomb.
They'll soon depart these shores. Stay safe and hidden."
It's easy to withstand their rum-filled bottles,
but just suppose these madmen carry cheese?

Thomas
(for Derek Walcott)

Another Malabar sunrise.
Encircling dunes and palms that bow to earth,
paying mock respect to me,
their sceptical Messiah.
I doubt tomorrow will arrive,
but I'm happy building sand-churches
that may outlast another tide.

I dream about an over-crowded day,
when He fed hundreds, maybe more.
I doubt there were five thousand – who can say? –
and the wine flowed freely, that's for sure.
James and John brought shoals of fishes from the nets
they'd kept away from public view
and there were scores of bakers at the back,
kneading the miracle with their hands,
while He, upfront, entranced the audience with his tales.

I'm not naïve, like trusting Joseph.
He pooh-poohed cynics who looked twice
and said his son was human,
though not a chip from his old block.
And chaste, unsullied Mary, she could tell a story.
She taught me how to talk the talk.
So, since I never saw Him rise
and wasn't there when others saw Him after "death",
when *she* was gone, I worked a wonder of my own,
and spun my tale of *her* ascent from earth.

Now supine on these gold blaspheming sands,
sun-blind, web-footed, waving scrolls amid the fronds,
I'll spread the faith, avoiding Galilean cant,
a new hot gospel, laced with Common Era doubt.
A hermit crab moves sideways near my feet,
my first disciple, writing hieroglyphics in the sand,
Reshaping all my words in his Dravidian scrawl.
I school myself to doubt my doubt.
I talk to roaches, get wisdom from mosquitoes.

I learn the tongues of my new land.

It's true I tried to touch the nail marks in His hands.
"Feeling is believing," a knowing Roman said.
But believing what? He'd always been so smart.
Perhaps he never died at all.
I see a figure underneath the palms.
I think it's Him, come searching for me here.
Quick. I must translate His message first.

Nosferatu

The vampire bats flew south last May.
We sighed and breathed routine again.

Now others will be drained by their nocturnal visits,
while we warn all our friends on Facebook,
who ask where they may next alight
and what we think of TV haemovores.

There will be peace in our virtual time,
but I dream of a future,
with blood, hate, healing and love.

Let the bloodsuckers return swiftly.

These are no ordinary vampires.
They've lost their way in daytime television,
anaemic mazes where the new shows seem repeats.
They come together late at night,
to say another lingering last goodbye
in this round room with jaded wooden panels
and worn-out folding metal chairs,
stacked close against its concave walls.
She strokes his cheek in fond, enfeebled hurt,
a gesture she may never make again.
He licks her neck, too weary now to bite.
Blood-red has turned to monochrome.
They've know each other far too long.

There's just one hope their vigour may return
through spectral reruns of the broadcasts of their days,
in which the outcomes change: the gameshows end in killings;
the talk show hosts fall silent; the antiques are all fake;
and liberation comes when knowing city couples
in search of homes with walled, protected gardens,
Horatian farms, Arcadian retreats,
are misdirected into Transylvanian hills.
They chuckle as they contemplate the prospect.
youth beckons with a crooked little finger;
anticipation quivers on their lips.

Courtly Love

Your mobile phone is static, your doorbell doesn't ring.
My frenzied knocking echoes down this street
of a thousand pairs of shrouded curtains,
but is it ever heard within your walls?
I must believe it's possible to get … near to you.

The sounds I hear mutate from hour to hour,
but seem to tell me of your many moods.
One voice is raucous and forbidding.
Another whispers secrets through the keyhole.
Chuckles promise shared intimacies.
Stifled sobs suggest that you may suffer too.
Then evening mutes these half-heard murmurings.
I keep my ear close to the ground by your locked door,
so that I can feel I am … near to you.

By the back gate I meet your feline shadow,
a green-eyed feral denizen of night,
who never deigns to argue, seldom comes for food,
but fights a ginger tom for rights of passage.
Disdainful he may be, obsessed with marking territories of home,
but I know that *he* is sometimes … near to you.

Peering through the lowest of your windows,
I watch your lapdog wag a friendly tail.
She must be close to you, though you remain unseen.
Yours is a house with sinuous corridors,
sealed rooms, closed shutters, wraithlike blinds.
You hide in attics, basements, turrets.
You take refuge in priest-holes from the past.

I clamber onto your roof and scrape my knee.
Avoiding your CCTV cameras,
I haul myself across your Roman tiles.
I try to spy you down your blocked-up chimney,
thinking that you may take pity on the blood
shed gladly in the hope of getting … near to you.

I wonder if you may have gone to sleep,
not knowing that your prince is close at hand,
or let your hair down from your tower and escaped,
to Laos, Colombia, or the land of Oz.

I fly a kite, with telescopic camera.
I raise the periscope from my pocket submarine in your lake.
I lap other runners circling the perimeter of your house.
I scythe through the weeds in your tangled garden.
Breathless, I climb an ancient knotted oak.
I dangle from a willow, risking limb and life.
I shovel earth, as I attempt to tunnel under your moat.
My one and only wish: to be … near to you.

Tempests

Narcissistic poets of the arbitrary,
for centuries they skirted seashores,
flirting lasciviously with the fragile hemlines
of landlocked maidens, chastened by their belts.
But now these fickle libertines
are drawn to fields exhausted by uncaring fumes.
They strive to penetrate unpapered former forests,
their lust unquenched by swamping fertile plains.

Reckless servants of a gambled carbon chance,
they level playing fields, raise roofs and flatten earth.
In former times they whispered courtship,
with warm plantation chaff upon their breath,
windborne jets of streaming passion from the Gulf.
They promised future-tense engagements,
but now those worn-out ways have been abandoned,
like the tattered remnants of a shipwrecked sailor's shirt.

Unleashing hail
on naked hamlets,
they drown ophelias
in their wanton rain.

Broad-shouldered men build arks of gopher
and hurry zebras up their ramps.
Sharks give gorillas swimming lessons.
Where costs allow, big cats have them too.
Meteorology floods all the channels.
The world looks upwards for a rainbow;
weatherwomen long for more monsoons.

The Natural Order

In the desert, camels were grouping to attack alien troops.
Fish were leaping from the ocean to protest about submarines.
Crows were swooping from the sky to peck at landmines.
In the forest, apes were surrendering their dreams of becoming men.

A parliament of fowls voted to declare independence.
A school of whales decided to abandon the classroom.

A dryad was pleased to be a tree.
Lot's wife rejoiced to be turned to stone.
Ganesh pricked up his elephant ears.
Hanuman deserted Rama and joined the apes.

Afterwards

This is a book club with no readers.
There is a garden with no flowers.
This is a country without leaders,
where I while away twilight-red hours.

This is the lost world of my boyhood.
There is the place where I was born.
This is the paper from the wildwood,
pages of forests, leafless and torn.

Here is the tip where we'd recycle.
This is the bin we christened our own.
There is the broken-armed doll of your girlhood,
tilting her head with a question: "Alone?"

And here is the fallout from a wandering sandstorm,
covering our treasures, our relics, our rust.
You always said that *I* was the dreamer,
but you were the one who succumbed to the dust.

There is the shrine to your sudden convulsion,
its letters worn weary with premature age.
I come to worship, consumed with revulsion,
wordlessly trying to muster some rage.

Uncle

As my pimpled nephew's kite soars sunwards
in a tangled, looping, long ambitious arc,
my unblinking eyes follow, never losing track.
I tell him all is well, no need to worry,
although it's heading for the phone wires.
If they snag it, I can scale poles –
I took a climbing course in eastern France.

Tomorrow there's the match with Chelsea,
which, he's heard, the pundits think we'll lose.
I find statistics, proving they're quite wrong,
and anyway there's often heroism in defeat.
He still thinks that winning proves you're better.
I say we always live to fight another day.

But yesterday he found out life is not forever.
We held a quiet, formal garden service,
a matchstick cross, a jamjar coffin packed with rice,
and prayed that Spudzy would find friends in hamster heaven.
I told my nephew he'll fly higher than the kite.

Out in the street we see a blackened limo,
heading a fragile convoy of dejected cars.
My nephew asks about the meaning of a hearse.
I say it carries people to a fairground
of Ferris wheels that spin eternally,
just like the one that took my sister to the skies,
the mother he was still too young to know.

Grandmother

I

"I'll gladly tell you all about her,
if you have five minutes you can spare.

"She sat there in that seat – yes, that chair there –
quietly knitting her memories of the war.
The Great one? Yes. The Second one as well.
In her final years, retired, though not before she had to,
she spent her days on this back porch, sunburnt,
stroked by rays that splintered through the glass,
just there. Yes, through *that* large pane –
they shone through that one over there.

"And earlier? Well, that's another story.
a bursting bag of sewing, sprouts and seeds.
But here … she sat and hardly moved at all,
except to walk her frame down to the bathroom,
ten yards at most along the half-lit hall.

"I asked her once what moment she recalled most
from her crowded life of rarebits, trifles, stews.
She'd had a stroke and giggled, coughed and spluttered:
'Women bus conductors in the first of those big wars.'

"More detail? You'd like to know my feelings
and hear my potted bio of her life.
You're not too bored by what I'm saying?
OK, here goes. I'll tell you what I can,
part truth, part rumour and the rest is fiction,
my best guess, but I think I'm mostly right."

II

"Towards the end her body seemed quite flattened,
like the flowers pressed into her herbal,
a browned Edwardian cornucopia,
kept close beside the Bible of her cookbook,
a talisman with recipes she knew by heart.

I wonder who will ever make them now.

"Her coffin was quite plain, in no way special,
no hint of her abounding life
that burst the seams of those who would contain her.
I can't believe she won't be here tonight.

"Her floral apron housed so many keepsakes,
its pockets crammed with spices, charms and pins.
Was she really once a cook
in one of those vast mansions
on the outer edge of Regent's Park,
a downstairs life lived just beneath the 'great'?
That's what they said. A letter proves it's likely.
Her husband's script on crumbling paper.
His clumsy billet-doux, his litany of flattery,
penned in his pride. He had a way with words.
I see her reading it by gaslight,
too wise to take him at face value,
too poor to spurn him without further thought.

"I see them meet at Speakers' Corner
to stroll down Hyde Park's democratic paths,
an unrestricted garden of desire.
Penny deckchairs basking in the sunshine,
hand-holding, serpentining walks.

"And, after marriage? I see her cornered in his sweetshop,
submissive to the watchword of his business:
'The customer is always right.'
He built a large newspaper empire
and sold his goods across the lines of class,
and she was always, always cooking
for the stomach-marching army of his staff.

"And sometimes there were three-day breaks in Brighton
in tacky bed-and-breakfasts near the piers,
with rock and candy floss and Lucie Attwell.
He loved all this. She waited to go home.

"They said she was 'a poor soul, to be pitied.

He went with other women, and she knew.'
I see her smiling at this eggshell gossip,
easy for her to crack, but better left alone.
As if she cared. Why would she care?
Just glad to have him anywhere but home.

She taught us how to manage skills that mattered:
poach eggs, play draughts, eat jelly, wash behind our ears,
and seal his letters with his heated orange wax.
She fed stray cats, put milk out for a hedgehog,
inclined her head to let her mongrel lick her ears,
and taught my brother's parrot how to swear.
And how she cared, how much she cared.

"But most of all she baked and boiled and roasted,
fish pies, steamed cabbage, Scotch broth, mutton stews,
feeding all his staff – her own five thousand –
fresh miracles reconjured every day.

"She made our world secure and safe, unchanging.
She soothed our troubles, never voiced her own.
She read our thoughts before we even spoke them.
She solved our problems, cutting to the bone."

III

"I'd better stop. I really can't convey her.
This is her apron. Would you like to touch it?
This is her photo. Do you like her smile?
Her chair? No please leave that alone."

Another Night

I dream Scheherazade is whispering night-time tales
to Aboriginal piscivores,
who squat by rockpools on an Alpine ridge.
There seems to be no danger from the snows,
nor threat of injury from human hand,
but, babbling storyteller that she is,
she chatters on to prove that she's alive.

She yawns, and then the horseshoe moon goes down,
and cobalt night gives way to saffron dawn.
She dozes, wakes and starts to talk again.
At times her absent-minded listeners hear her words,
half with her, while they fish and chat and paint.
Their splattered watches may be fast or slow;
a GPS is lost in boundless space.
The dreamtime tale is left suspended
in the static balance of a sun-blind world.

It is the storyteller's perfect moment,
as the urgency of narrative
drifts into an aimless present,
losing itself in the ripples of the pool.
The impetus towards conclusion disappears
and death is thwarted by the glaciers of the day.

Body Politic

I aspire to become a coalition.
My amiable arms reach out to hug my cheerful chest.
My running eyes observe my legs with tears of love.
But still I have rebellious digits,
tepid toes and fugitive fingers,
refusing orders sent from up above.

So sometimes I succumb to thoughts of separation,
weary to know that after years of talking truces,
ceasefires and peace, so much remains undone.
Federation is still a distant pipe-dream.
My knees have formed a power bloc of their own.

Walking Poem

This poem walks down the street
on a seven-inch tablet,
full of HD light and slender poise.
This is an ambitious poem:
it wants to be flashed around the world
as an instant tweeted message
about the Pope and peace and politics,
but it starts to get too long.
It needs to take a taxi home,
to a laptop or a desktop screen.
or an anxious sheet of paper,
where, immaculately conceived,
it fears it may never be read.

Imaginings flowed freely all that summer,
between the north and south, the west and east.
They travelled downwards, upwards, sideways, all ways,
striving to reach far corners of the globe.

Acned George, in England's Kentish garden,
dug twisting holes to reach the land of Oz.
hard labour for a skinny ten-year-old.
Adjourning every evening when the light failed,
he recommenced his work next day at dawn,
his goal Cassandra, living "down" in Melbourne,
unknown to George, a woman in her prime.
She texted him: no earth had moved as yet
and, lacking faith, embraced her namesake's gloom.

On a vacant lot in Minnesota,
Priscilla moved soft soil to journey east.
Her cravings nurtured first by *The Mikado*,
she tunnelled, singing songs from *Miss Saigon*.
She knew that China lay within her reach.
She'd get there if she burrowed long enough.
She'd learn karate from a black-belt warlord
and read Confucius with a bearded saint.
She'd chew chow mein, eat sweet and sour chicken,
she'd dip her egg roll in her wonton soup,
her wishes granted through Aladdin's lamp.

In a crowded town in Haryana,
coy Sita had no room at all to dig,
but she too reached another distant world
by sending messages to Augustin in Brussels.
He asked how she was coping with her exile,
now Rama had despatched her to the woods.
He was, his messages implied, au fait with all things Asian,
though, truth be told, he'd never strayed from home.
He'd read the *Ramayana* – in more than one translation,
though she hadn't yet found out exactly which.

Too well-bred to be openly flirtatious,
she laced her emails with emojis,
the smiley ones, so easy to insert.
She played his game, and answered him with irony:
no hurry to come riding to her rescue,
she loved her canopy of forest foliage,
the tigers, earthworms, crocodiles and crows.
All creatures pleased her gentle Hindu soul!

Cassandra dodged her Melbourne suburb's showers,
to reach the pawn shop down the road,
texted her ageing mother back in Athens,
to say she'd send her money very soon.
Yes, it *was* winter, but she wasn't cold.
No time to dream of other places,
she had to sell her jewellery and her gold.

From Dylan to Dylan

The ragman still draws circles.
He's been perfecting them for years,
around the pyramids of molehills
that hide his ashen fears.

A hearse is now approaching,
with pallid lowered beams,
on this highway of cracked asphalt,
the broken diamonds of his dreams.

His fires don't light swiftly
like the beacons of his youth,
but he keeps a dawn flame flickering,
so deaf spirits may hear truth.

Dusk is now descending,
on his caravan of light,
but he snared the sun at noon-time
and he'll rage against the night.

The Tortoisiad
(for Cruz Bonilla)

A small society of tortoises,
A rescued family of tortoisekind.

In the beginning was the shell,
a pristine perfect carapace,
or so the story goes – such human lies.
Then one day it got cracked and mottled,
in those fallen fantasies of Adam's kind.
They heard of tricksters tumbling down from heaven,
and wondered who these tales might be about.
They heard a fable linking them with Hare,
where slow and steady wins the race,
but, neither slow nor steady in their gait,
they did not recognise this might be them.
They stood stock still when placed beside a rabbit,
their only running was with one another,
when they moved faster than this crawling verse.

A ring-backed Ulysses watched TV flickers,
these silhouettes his world of ideal Forms.
Dormant through the day, he came alive at prime time,
his world determined by his owner's soapy tastes.
Far from Troy's embattled walls,
near the western reaches of that same sea,
where once his namesake travelled for a decade,
dallying with the sirens of the isles,
this Ulysses was shipwrecked in a box.
Then in the middle of the journey of his life,
emancipation came, with others of his kind,
his Ithaca a new-found seaside home.
Illumination now arose from other sources.
Venturing three metres to a balcony,
he'd keep an earnest evening vigil,
he'd gaze upon the lustre of the moon.

Sokrates once lived a nonchalant existence,
immune from social pride, beneath an Afric sun
that shone upon his perfect little pebbles,

filled in with dandelion, a bit of clover, cedar cones.
Spring came with its cruel flowing sap,
raising the urge for prey in an obedient hound,
and following the hound, a master's human hand!
His head was chewed, he dragged one foot behind him.
A crushed existence, ground down from then on,
he always links the dog, the man, the stone.
Behind him now, forever lost,
the foreign golden sands and turquoise sea
of what was once Saladin's dream.
He crossed the strait where Hercules had been before him,
survived the damaged plastron of the fight.
He has the wisdom of his namesake,
but cloaks this truth in hibernating night.

He slowly settled in his new Iberian clime,
a patriarch, without a dynasty, without a mate.
So nut-sized, rescued orphan Pepepillo,
an inbred bully from a septic plastic hell,
was brought to satisfy his spry desire.
But Pepe was no Helen, just another mooning male!
Nurtured until now on fish and food waste,
he turned to eating everything in sight.
He cleaned up wood, small specks of dirt and dustballs,
until Athena's guiding hand restored his health,
with spoonfed eggs and syringed yoghurt.
Emboldened by his newfound piglet strength,
alone, heroic, fearless, if misguided,
Pepe resolved to fight his own Homeric war.
Sokrates looked on amused, sagacious,
then deigned to grab the upstart by a leg
and threw the pixie warrior several metres.
Pepe's dream was shattered in an instant.
He knew he must withdraw from this lost fight.
With Sokrates he knew he must be humble,
a Sancho acting out the better part of valour,
a histrionic mimic of the knight.
Yet martial lust can be a fierce addiction.
He yearned to browbeat others of his kind,
and skirmishes became a daily drill.
Such is the lore of small chelonian life.

The family has a sweet and gentle member,
who seeks out favours, while he shares his own.
Rufino was the sole survivor of eleven,
hatched a year before they met their doom,
when wanton hunters in a one-time forest,
now swallowed by the town's insistent sprawl,
despoiled their nest, destroyed their only home.
Adrift, abandoned in a landlocked desert,
Rufino never fought in Trojan battles
but suffered all the aftermath of war.
Another foundling, much in need of refuge,
he, too, found safety in Athena's care.
His playful nature hides beneath small strips of cloth,
invisible to those he then can't see,
but once the world believes he's truly vanished
he reappears, with shiny smiling eyes
that say, "It's me. I've cheated you again."
He's ready now for food and loving touches,
his courage and his joy infect the house.

Now some would say it's just tautology,
to speak of all these varied tortoise types:
"A tortoise is a tortoise, have no doubt."
But every dappled hero tells a different story,
a tale that can't be spoken in this verse.
Each champion frustrates the snares of language
that tries to trap him in this slow *Tortoisiad*.

www.ingramcontent.com/pod-product-compliance
Lightning Source LLC
Chambersburg PA
CBHW071935020426
42331CB00010B/2878